The Greatest Song of All

How Isaac Stern United the World to Save Carnegie Hall

Written by **Megan Hoyt**   Illustrated by **Katie Hickey**

Quill Tree Books
An Imprint of HarperCollinsPublishers

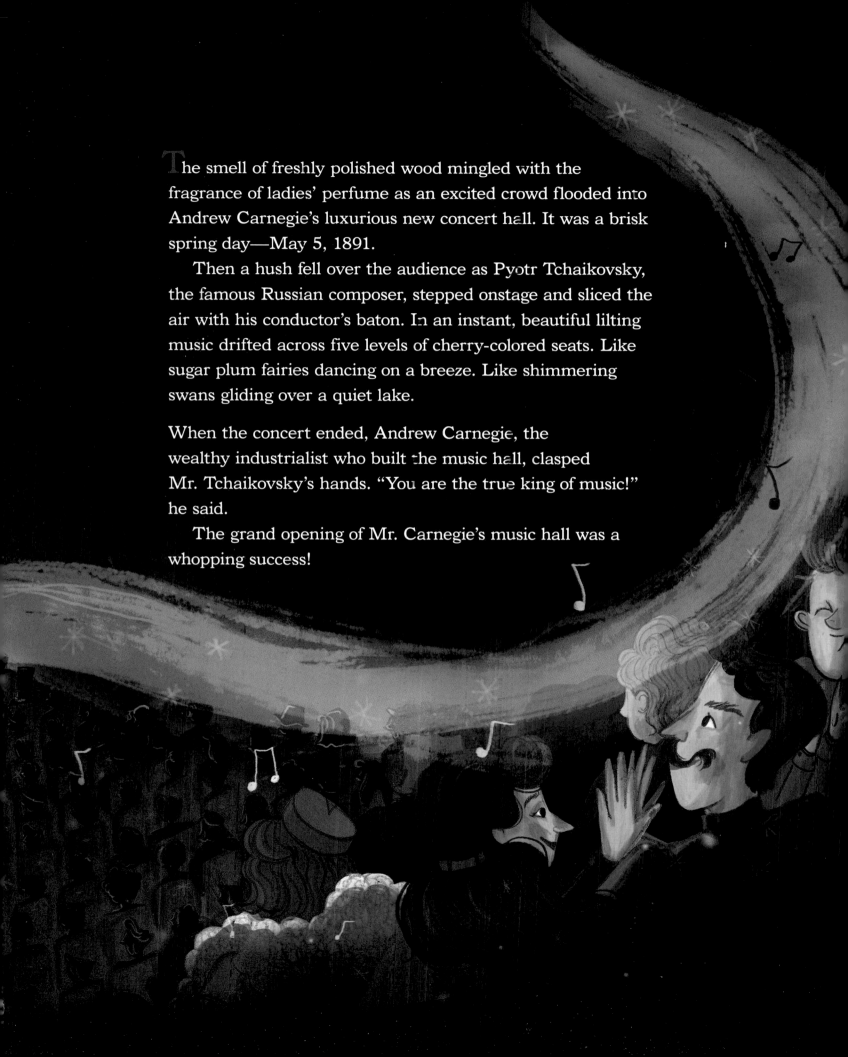

The smell of freshly polished wood mingled with the fragrance of ladies' perfume as an excited crowd flooded into Andrew Carnegie's luxurious new concert hall. It was a brisk spring day—May 5, 1891.

Then a hush fell over the audience as Pyotr Tchaikovsky, the famous Russian composer, stepped onstage and sliced the air with his conductor's baton. In an instant, beautiful lilting music drifted across five levels of cherry-colored seats. Like sugar plum fairies dancing on a breeze. Like shimmering swans gliding over a quiet lake.

When the concert ended, Andrew Carnegie, the wealthy industrialist who built the music hall, clasped Mr. Tchaikovsky's hands. "You are the true king of music!" he said.

The grand opening of Mr. Carnegie's music hall was a whopping success!

Soon other famous performers lined up to make their Carnegie Hall debuts. Jazz musicians and ballet dancers. Classical composers and concert violinists.

Marian Anderson wowed the audience with her powerful voice, smooth and deep.

Duke Ellington jazzed up the crowd with his rich bass tones and tinkling trebles.

Albert Einstein spoke about splitting atoms and bending time.

$E = MC^2$

Carnegie Hall welcomed artists of all skin colors, religions, and wealth. Every difference melted away the moment the curtains opened and music drifted across the air.

But someone new would soon step onto the legendary stage. Without him, Carnegie Hall's story might have ended right here. His name was Isaac Stern.

While Albert Einstein was mesmerizing the crowd at Carnegie Hall, Isaac Stern was still screeching out simple tunes on a secondhand violin. Gradually, the instrument began to obey his slender fingers, and soon brisk notes slipped from his bedroom window and bounced across the choppy San Francisco Bay.

His parents marveled at his progress. As Jewish immigrants escaping the tragedies of war-torn Ukraine, they had come to San Francisco with almost nothing. They scrimped and saved until pennies became dollars. Then they sent their son to the best violin teacher in town.

Still, Carnegie Hall seemed like a far-off dream for nine-year-old Isaac. But he knew from watching his parents that you must never give up on your dreams!

He practiced for hours every day for many years.

He performed all over town and even on a
radio broadcast. Then it happened. . . .

An agent in New York City invited Isaac to
perform in a special recital.

It was finally time.

Isaac Stern was headed to Carnegie Hall!

His stomach filled with butterflies as he warmed up in a rehearsal room, coaxing each note out of the violin with confidence.

Then Isaac planted his feet on Carnegie's gleaming stage, and magnificent music poured from his violin.

The audience was spellbound.

Years drifted past. Isaac performed at Carnegie Hall more than fifty times. He fell in love with the enormous auditorium, with its brilliant acoustics and crisp sound. This cavernous ruby-colored room felt like a second home to Isaac.

"This is *my* room," he said. And it was.

In fact, every time he walked into the hall, his love
for the magnificent building grew. He could hear history
whisper through its hallways—the hum of Ukrainian folk
songs from his childhood mixed with the overtures of
famous conductors.

Isaac was happy. Content. At peace.

He didn't know it yet, but he was about to
face the biggest battle of his life—the fight
to save Carnegie Hall.

Powerful city planner Robert Moses was sweeping through
Manhattan, demolishing neighborhoods, bulldozing parks, and
rearranging the city as if its buildings were pieces on a chessboard.
His job was to get rid of old, unsightly buildings and modernize
Manhattan. His mind swirled with grids and sketches and plans.
It may have looked like he was making the city more beautiful,
but when Mr. Moses decided Manhattan needed a new, bigger
music hall, he didn't mind knocking down eighteen city blocks
to make room for it.

And what about the elegant Carnegie Hall a few blocks away?
People might choose to go to a Carnegie performance instead of one
at his sleek new Lincoln Center! Mr. Moses would have to demolish
Carnegie Hall too.

Deals were made. Plans were drawn up. A demolition crew was
hired, and the date was set.

Carnegie Hall would meet the wrecking ball on March 31, 1960.

When Isaac first heard the news, he could hardly believe it. Then his shock turned to anger. This could not happen to his beloved building! The news spread quickly, and soon hundreds of people gathered in front of Carnegie Hall, right in the middle of 57th Street, to protest.

Ballet dancers leaped and danced.
Musicians performed.
Elderly music lovers linked arms with young children.
"STOP THE WRECKING BALL!" they shouted. "Save Carnegie Hall!"

But the next day, the people of New York City went back to their daily routines. Cars and buses cruised past the hall, pouring exhaust and dirt onto the sidewalk out front.

Isaac looked around. Didn't they know this was where the famous Tchaikovsky made his American debut? Where Albert Einstein mesmerized the crowd with his talk of tiny atoms in a vast universe? Where the lilting tones of Marian Anderson melted people's hearts?

Just like Isaac, young musicians from all over the world dreamed of one day performing at the prestigious Carnegie Hall.

It has to be saved, Isaac thought.

So Isaac got to work. He contacted Robert Wagner Jr., the mayor of New York City, and asked how much it would cost to save Carnegie Hall. He almost fell out of his chair when he heard the answer: five million dollars! Isaac Stern was not a millionaire. He was a violinist. How would he ever raise that much money?

But he pushed ahead and he, along with former usher John Totten, former first lady Eleanor Roosevelt, and other concerned music lovers, formed a committee to save Carnegie Hall.

They placed ads in newspapers and on the radio.

Children emptied their piggy banks.

Musicians performed benefit concerts.

But they were very far from their goal.

Famous performers still lined up to make their Carnegie debuts. Jazz musicians and ballet dancers. Classical composers and concert violinists. Except now, every performer who stepped onstage wondered if this would be their last Carnegie Hall performance. Isaac wondered too.

Meanwhile, a few blocks away, Robert Moses was pressing forward with his plan to build Lincoln Center. Before he could even break ground on the project, he would have to tear down every building in his way.

Neighbors peeked through closed curtains as thousands of families were pushed out onto the streets with nowhere to go.

Isaac was watching too.
I need a bigger plan, he
thought. *A GIANT plan.*

So Isaac got to work again. He contacted the most famous performers he knew—every big-name celebrity who had ever set foot on Carnegie's stage—and asked them to sign a petition. He took the petitions to Mayor Wagner, along with a plan that would allow New York City *itself* to buy Carnegie Hall.

"It's not just a piece of real estate," Isaac said. "For the musicians of the entire world, New York and Carnegie Hall and the United States— it's all one thing!"

Mayor Wagner told Isaac they would need to change the laws of New York in order to purchase Carnegie Hall. And even if the laws were changed in time, they did *not* have five million dollars.

It would take a miracle.

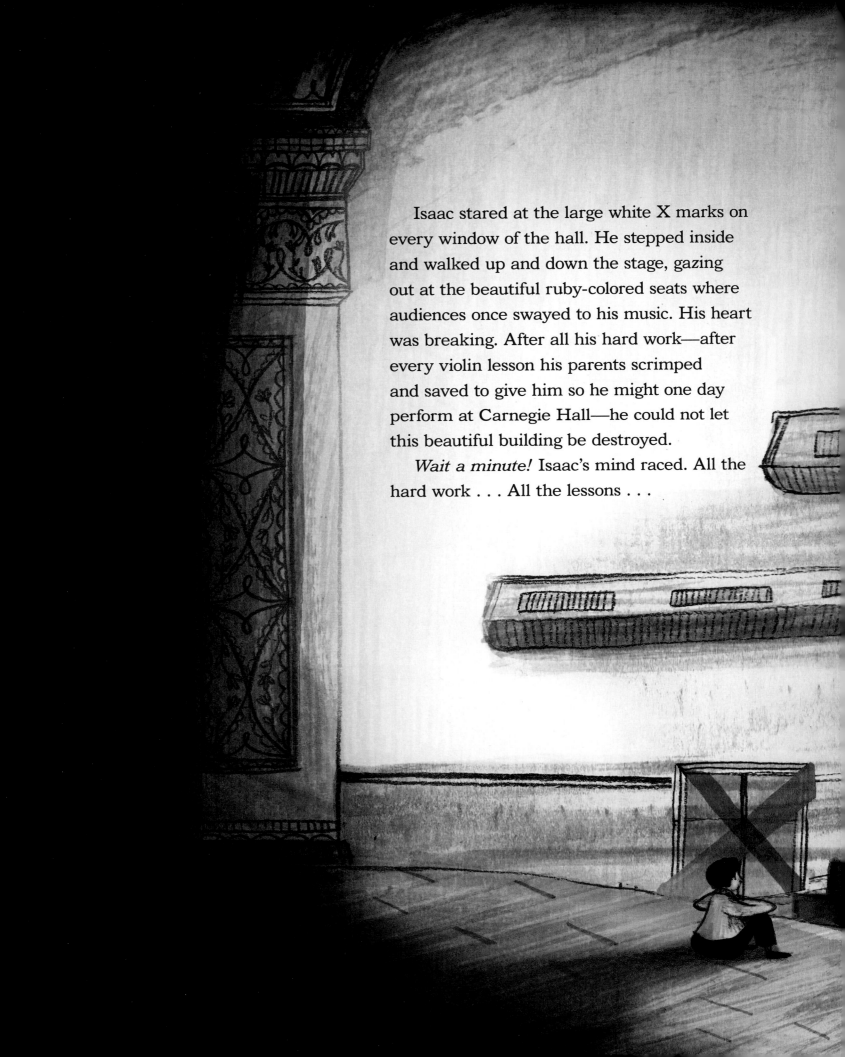

Isaac stared at the large white X marks on
every window of the hall. He stepped inside
and walked up and down the stage, gazing
out at the beautiful ruby-colored seats where
audiences once swayed to his music. His heart
was breaking. After all his hard work—after
every violin lesson his parents scrimped
and saved to give him so he might one day
perform at Carnegie Hall—he could not let
this beautiful building be destroyed.

Wait a minute! Isaac's mind raced. All the
hard work . . . All the lessons . . .

Why didn't he think of this before? Carnegie Hall would make a fabulous center for music education! Children could learn from the best teachers in the world!

Like a beautiful symphony,
ideas twisted and twirled
through Isaac's head.

This could be the greatest
song of all!

Isaac called every wealthy businessman
he could think of. He chatted with famous
millionaires at high-society parties. He
even asked Governor Nelson Rockefeller
for a donation. Isaac made so many phone
calls that people began to tease him, saying
that the phone was permanently attached
to his ear. But he did not give up.

Just one more call, he thought.

Then he found his miracle.

A wealthy New York businessman named Jacob Kaplan was happy to help. Mr. Kaplan's family owned the Welch's grape juice company. Children loved his grape juice, and Jacob Kaplan loved children. He thought saving Carnegie Hall was a splendid idea, and he thought turning it into a center for music education was an even better one.

He agreed to make a large donation. Isaac was thrilled!
Isaac and Jacob Kaplan formed a new committee—the
Citizen's Committee for Carnegie Hall. They got straight
to work, drawing up contracts and figuring out how the
hall could pay for itself, day after day, month
after month, year after year . . . *forever*!

But now it was a race against time.

Unless Mayor Wagner could convince the legislature to change the laws of New York quickly, Carnegie Hall would *still* be demolished in only a few days.

Music lovers around the world waited as members of the New York State Legislature cast their votes—would they allow New York City to purchase Carnegie Hall and rent it to Isaac Stern and his benefactors?

YES!
Carnegie Hall was SAVED!

Isaac's heart was bursting with joy. "When you believe in something, you can move mountains!" he said.

Once again, Carnegie Hall opened its doors to talented performers from all over the world—rich and poor, young and old, American-born or immigrants seeking a better life, like Isaac Stern's family did many years ago.

AUTHOR'S NOTE

Megan Hoyt inside the legendary Carnegie Hall

New York City concert halls have a special place in my heart for one very important reason—they are where my parents first met! Both were symphony musicians who regularly played in pit orchestras around town. My mother was a violinist like Isaac Stern, and my father played the viola and French horn.

Back when my parents lived in New York, during the 1940s, there was no air-conditioning in the old concert halls. During those hot summer months in the orchestra pit, my father kept smelling salts on his music stand. When he saw my mother beginning to sway, growing faint from the heat, he would reach over and revive her with the strong smell of these salts.

After a concert one evening, for their first official date, my parents strolled over to the nearby Carnegie Deli for cheesecake. My father never shared food with anyone, but he shared his cheesecake with my mother that night.

The rest, as they say, is history. *My* history.

As I started to do research on Carnegie Hall, I went to the source: the hall itself! There are hundreds of letters, photos, and contracts tucked away in the Carnegie Hall archives, including an autographed photo of Tchaikovsky—composer of *The Nutcracker* and *Swan Lake*—and the trowel Louise Carnegie used back in 1890 to lay the first cornerstone of the building. I was given a backstage tour and taken to the museum after hours to photograph everything I needed to tell Isaac's story. Isaac Stern also left dozens of boxes of relevant background information to the US government. They are stored in the National Archives and have not yet been opened. Maybe one day we will find out even more about Carnegie Hall, about Isaac Stern, and about the activism that saved this beautiful building from destruction.

—M.H.

MORE ABOUT CARNEGIE HALL

When wealthy financier Andrew Carnegie and his wife, Louise, set sail for Scotland on their honeymoon, they met Walter Damrosch, the director of the Oratorio Society of New York, the city's first music association. Maybe it was the sea breeze or the salty air, but as they rocked gently along, Mr. Damrosch grew bold enough to share his vision for a new concert hall in New York City. By the time they reached Scotland, Mr. Carnegie had decided to build it.

When Louise laid the first stone of Carnegie Hall into the ground in 1890, her husband said, "It is built to stand for ages, and during these ages it is probable that this hall will intertwine itself with the history of our country." It certainly has—welcoming famous composers and opera singers, jazz greats like Duke Ellington and Dizzy Gillespie, and even rock and roll superstars like Bob Dylan and the Beatles.

The acoustics at Carnegie Hall were perfect, and that was no accident. The architect who built it, William Tuthill, was a cello player. The heavy velvet, the curved box seating, the hole in the ceiling—they all contributed to the hall's rich reverb and silky sound.

Jazz artist Louis Armstrong playing the trumpet at Carnegie Hall

Carnegie Hall seated 2,804 people. That was enormous by 1890s standards. But audiences filled the hall night after night. It was the place to "be seen" for high-society New Yorkers, and a steady stream of famous performers lined up to perform on Carnegie's main stage. The same is true today.

But Robert Moses did not particularly care for fancy architecture or historic monuments. He only wanted to eradicate run-down buildings and keep traffic flowing. Moses was a civil engineer—someone who plans how a city will be built, what architecture is allowed, and what laws need to be passed in order to make sure everything runs smoothly.

When he decided to build Lincoln Center, he needed to demolish sixty acres. That meant throwing forty thousand people out of their homes. *Forty thousand!* Can you imagine that many people trying to find a new place to live all at the same time, in the same city? In 1960, the San Juan Hill neighborhood where Robert Moses set his stakes to put Lincoln Center was home to mostly Black families working two or three jobs, scrimping and saving to make ends meet, struggling to feed their families. Most of them lived in squalid conditions in the depths of poverty. They had little time to prepare or seek new housing, and only a few thousand received help from the city to find shelter.

Lincoln Square residents protesting Carnegie's demolition

Saving Carnegie Hall was tricky, but Isaac Stern was great at convincing people to help. He was a fantastic community organizer as well as a talented concert violinist. But he needed business smarts to figure out the rental contracts and laws surrounding such a huge transaction. One of his first allies in the project was Mayor Robert Wagner, who he met at a Jewish Passover Seder. After talking late into the night about various ways to solve the money problem, Mayor Wagner agreed to be the go-between and help Isaac understand the legal procedures and how to deal with changing laws within the New York State Legislature. Jacob Kaplan provided the funds for renovations and joined the committee soon after it was formed. Once the laws were changed and the city was allowed to purchase Carnegie Hall and rent it to Isaac's committee, the rest was left to lawyers and contract negotiators. How much rent would they pay? How long would the lease last? Isaac was concerned that the same thing could happen all over again once the lease expired. He fought to make Carnegie Hall a National Historic Landmark. Now no one will ever be able to destroy it.

Carnegie Hall opens its doors to performers of all ages, from all walks of life and all backgrounds. Like the Statue of Liberty, it stands as a monument to everything that is good and true about the United States of America. Religion, skin color, and social status melt away once the music begins, and resounding applause rises equally for everyone. That is the power of music. That is the elegant activism of Carnegie Hall.

Carnegie Hall today

MORE ABOUT ISAAC STERN

When Isaac Stern was born in 1920, Jewish people in Russia-controlled Ukraine, where he and his parents lived, were not treated well. His parents saved up enough money to flee the persecution and poverty they were experiencing and start a new life in San Francisco, California. It was good that they did. Not one family member who remained in their hometown of Kreminiecz, Ukraine, survived the Holocaust that was to come two decades later in 1941 during World War II. In fact, out of a Jewish population of fifteen thousand, only fourteen Jewish people in Kreminiecz survived the Holocaust.

Isaac's journey to Carnegie Hall was not easy. Once he and his parents stepped off the boat in San Francisco, his father, Solomon Stern, found work painting houses, and his mother, Clara Stern, taught music lessons. She had been a popular singer back in Ukraine, but in San Francisco they were newly arrived immigrants struggling to make ends meet any way they could. When his teacher realized he had immense talent, Isaac was invited to perform on a radio broadcast, and a top New York agent, Sol Hurok, showed interest in representing him. Sol brought him to Carnegie Hall for his debut, and Isaac's popularity soared. He performed for presidents, traveled back to Soviet Russia to perform in his former homeland and to China, and even performed in Israel during a raid while the audience donned gas masks. He was filled with relentless courage, a passion for music, and a love for children. Whether hobnobbing with movie stars and presidents or playing for his grandchildren at home, Isaac Stern was a gift to the United States of America as much as his new home country was a gift to him.

TIMELINE

May 5, 1891 Grand opening concert, conducted by Pyotr Tchaikovsky

December 30, 1928 Marian Anderson, contralto performance

April 1, 1934 Albert Einstein is honored at Carnegie Hall.

January 8, 1943 Isaac Stern makes his Carnegie Hall debut.

September 29, 1947 Dizzy Gillespie, Charlie Parker, and Ella Fitzgerald make their jazz debut.

December 1959 There is a meeting at Jacob Kaplan's house to discuss saving Carnegie Hall. Kaplan, a wealthy financier, made his money from Welch's grape juice.

January 10, 1960 The Citizen's Committee for Carnegie Hall holds its first meeting at Isaac Stern's apartment. They requested help from Governor Nelson Rockefeller—he refused.

Feb 2, 1960 There is a larger group meeting at Jacob Kaplan's home. Isaac Stern was to write a letter to the mayor, Robert E. Wagner Jr., requesting political assistance, but family illness and a tour prevented him from moving forward.

March 11, 1960 Isaac Stern sends a telegram to Mayor Wagner offering to create a youth orchestra and begging for help to ensure that "one of the few acoustically perfect concert halls" is not removed from the international music scene.

Demolition is rescheduled for May 1960.

March 30, 1960 With only days left in the state legislative session, Isaac Stern meets with Mayor Wagner to create legislation. Astonishingly, it is voted on three days later.

April 11, 1960 Isaac Stern attends a Passover Seder and is seated next to Mayor Wagner. He invites the mayor over to his apartment and further explains the urgency of saving Carnegie Hall. The mayor agrees with him.

April 16, 1960 Governor Rockefeller signs both bills into law. Now the government can purchase Carnegie Hall and rent it back to the Committee. Carnegie Hall is saved!

1964 Carnegie Hall is declared a National Historic Landmark.

April 1991 Carnegie Hall's 100th birthday

September 23–24, 2000 Carnegie Hall celebrates Isaac Stern's 80th birthday.

2009 Carnegie Hall brings music workshops to inmates at Sing Sing Correctional Facility.

2011 Studio Towers is renovated to provide more classrooms for music education.

2019 Family Day—children sing and dance with professional musicians.

THE PETITION WRITTEN BY ISAAC STERN

This petition was signed by twenty internationally known musicians
who all believed, like Isaac, that Carnegie Hall was worth saving.

I affirm my belief in the importance of keeping Carnegie Hall as a permanent cultural monument.

It is of historical significance in the musical development of the United States, the embodiment of our musical heritage. This is a consecrated house. It holds memories of all the great performances of all the world's great artists shared by many generations of music lovers.

Leaving aside all sentimental reasons, Carnegie Hall, for the world outside the United States, has become the symbol of the greatest achievements in music. In the minds of civilized men everywhere it is the gateway to musical America. To destroy it now for "practical reasons" is an act of irresponsibility damaging to the United States and our prestige in the entire civilized world.

Every great city in other countries has several concert halls and opera houses. For this reason we welcome the creation of Lincoln Center as an addition to our musical life. But Carnegie Hall must remain to serve the needs of an ever increasing musical public and as an inspiration and home for the development of the musicians of tomorrow.

(Signed)

Pablo Casals

Vladimir Horowitz

Jascha Heifetz Myra Hess Fritz Kreisler

Charles Munch Gregor Piatigorsky Arthur Rubinstein Leopold Stokowski

Leonard Bernstein Van Cliburn Dimitri Mitropoulos George Szell

Bruno Walter Mischa Elman

Mieczyslaw Horszowski Eugene Istomin

Erica Morini Nathan Milstein

SOURCES

Letters and newspaper clippings from the Carnegie Hall Archive and interviews with archivists Rob Hudson and Gino Francesconi.

Phone interviews and email correspondence with representatives from Carnegie Hall.

Carnegie Hall. The A to Z of Carnegie Hall: I Is for Irreplaceable. www.carnegiehall.org/Blog/2012/08/The-A-to-Z-of-Carnegie-Hall-I-is-for-Irreplaceable.

Carnegie Hall. Education. www.carnegiehall.org/Education.

Carnegie Hall. Timeline. www.carnegiehall.org/About/History/Timeline#1940s.

Ephemeral New York, "When Carnegie Hall Almost Met the Wrecking Ball," March 21, 2001. www.ephemeralnewyork.wordpress.com/2011/03/21/when-carnegie-hall-almost-met-the-wrecking-ball.

Farrell, Ben. "Fiddling Around: Isaac Stern and Comedian Jack Benny Play Bach at Carnegie Hall," WQXR Editorial, July 21, 2018. www.wqxr.org/story/isaac-stern-jack-benny-carnegie-hall.

Google Arts and Culture. "The Birth of Carnegie Hall." https://artsandculture.google.com/exhibit/the-birth-of-carnegie-hall-carnegie-hall/xwLSGVw2XO2JKQ?hl=en.

Green, David B. "This Day in Jewish History: 1920: Isaac Stern, Violinst Who Couldn't Play in Germany, Is Born," Haaretz, July 20, 2015. www.haaretz.com/jewish/.premium-1920-isaac-stern-is-born-1.5376879.

Haifetz, Jascha. "100 Years Ago Today: Heifetz's US Debut at Carnegie Hall," the Strad, October 27, 2017. www.thestrad.com/artists-old/100-years-ago-today-heifetzs-us-debut-at-carnegie- hall/7238.article.

Kozinn, Allan. "Violinist Isaac Stern Dies at 81; Led Efforts to Save Carnegie Hall," *New York Times*, September 23, 2001. www.nytimes.com/2001/09/23/nyregion/violinist-isaac-stern-dies-at-81-led-efforts-to-save-carnegie-hall.html.

Nestor, Matt. "Vintage Photos: The Lost San Juan Hill, Lincoln Center and a West Side Story," Untapped New York, March 19, 2014. www.untappedcities.com/2014/03/19/vintage-photos-the-lost-san-juan-hill-lincoln-center-and-a-west-side-story.

Reynolds, Christopher. "Step Inside New York's Carnegie Hall, Where Beautiful Music and Stirring History Ring Out," *Los Angeles Times*, March 23, 2018. www.latimes.com/travel/la-tr-carnegie-hall-20180325-htmlstory.html.

Roddy, Joseph. "Violinist Isaac Stern Is a Unique Virtuoso: He Plays Both Music and Politics with Rare Skill," *People*, January 13, 1977. www.people.com/archive/violinist-isaac-stern-is-a-unique-virtuoso-he-plays-both-music-and-politics-with-rare-skill-vol-7-no-4.

Ross, Alex. "Coming Apart," *The New Yorker*, March 25, 2002. www.newyorker.com/magazine/2002/04/01/coming-apart.

Schmitz and Elizabeth. "Saving Carnegie Hall: A Case Study of Historic Preservation in Postwar New York City," University of California–Riverside, June 2015. www.escholarship.org/uc/item/3x19f20h.

Stern, Isaac (written with Chaim Potok), *My First 79 Years*, Da Capo Press, 1999.

Sweeney, Louise. "Isaac Stern Concertmaster of the World," *Christian Science Monitor*, October 2, 1980. www.csmonitor.com/1980/1002/100251.html.

Weeks, Linton. "12 Lost American Slangisms from the 1800s," NPR, July 21, 2015. www.npr.org/sections/npr-history-dept/2015/07/21/423297371/12-lost-american-slangisms-from-the-1800s.

Wood, Anthony C., *Preserving New York: Winning the Right to Protect a City's Landmarks*, New York: Routledge, 2008.

Young, Michelle. "The Top 10 Secrets of Carnegie Hall in NYC," Untapped New York, June 4, 2015. www.untappedcities.com/2015/06/04/the-top-10-secrets-of-carnegie-hall-in-nyc/11.

For my parents, Michael and Nancy Glass,
who taught me to appreciate the beauty and
grandeur of magnificent concert halls.
–M.H.

For Jim x
–K.H.

Many thanks to Carnegie Hall archivists Gino Francesconi and Rob Hudson,
for their invaluable research assistance, and to William B. Tuthill, cellist and
architect, for designing the timeless masterpiece, Carnegie Hall.

Quill Tree Books is an imprint of HarperCollins Publishers.

The Greatest Song of All: How Isaac Stern United the World to Save Carnegie Hall
Text copyright © 2022 by Megan Hoyt
Illustrations copyright © 2022 by Katie Hickey
Photographs: pages 34 and 36: courtesy of Megan Hoyt; page 35: (Louis Armstrong)
William P. Gottlieb/Ira and Leonore S. Gershwin Fund Collection, Music Division,
Library of Congress; (picketing) Residents picket Astor . . . / *World Telegram*
& Sun photo by Phil Stanziola. New York, 1956. Photograph.

ISBN 978-0-06-304527-9

The artist used gouache, coloring pencil, and Photoshop
to create the digital illustrations for this book.
Lettering by Leah Palmer Preiss
Typography by Rachel Zegar
22 23 24 25 26   RTLO   10 9 8 7 6 5 4 3 2 1
❖
First Edition